OTHER GIFTBOOKS IN THIS SERIES
happy day!   *love*
hope! dream!   *smile*

Printed simultaneously in 2003 by Helen Exley Giftbooks
in Great Britain and Helen Exley Giftbooks LLC in the USA.

12 11 10

Illustrations © Joanna Kidney 2003
Copyright © Helen Exley 2003
The moral right of the author has been asserted.

ISBN 13: 978-1-86187-562-4

Edited by Helen Exley
Pictures by Joanna Kidney

Printed in China

Helen Exley Giftbooks, 16 Chalk Hill, Watford, Herts WD19 4BG, UK.

www.helenexleygiftbooks.com

friend

PICTURES BY JOANNA KIDNEY

The only secret was the ancient
communication between two people.

EUDORA WELTY (1909–2001)

FRIENDSHIP
CAN ONLY BE MEASURED
IN MEMORIES,
LAUGHTER,
PEACE AND LOVE.

STUART AND LINDA MACFARLANE

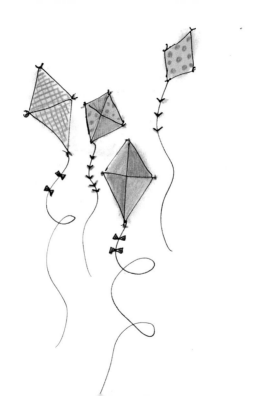

Friends do not live in harmony
merely, as some say,
but in melody.

HENRY DAVID THOREAU (1817–1862)

In prosperity a pleasure,
a solace in adversity, in grief a comfort,
in joy a merry companion,
at all times
an other I.

JOHN LYLY (1544–1606)

A friend is the bridge
into a wider world.

We see through their eyes as well
as through our own.
We listen more intently,
think more deeply, explore a country
we had never known.
We need their care and kindness –
and find delight in discovering
they need us too.

CHARLOTTE GRAY, B.1937

When two people
are at one in their inmost hearts,
They shatter even
the strength of iron or bronze.
And when two people
understand each other
in their inmost hearts,
Their words
are sweet and strong,
like the fragrance of orchids.

I CHING

I'm not strong. She's not strong.

But together

my friend and I

make the strongest force

in the known universe.

LINDA MACFARLANE

Two people,
yes, two lasting friends,
The giving comes,
the taking ends.
There is no measure
for such things,
For this all Nature
slows and sings.

ELIZABETH JENNINGS, (1926-2001),
FROM "FRIENDSHIP"

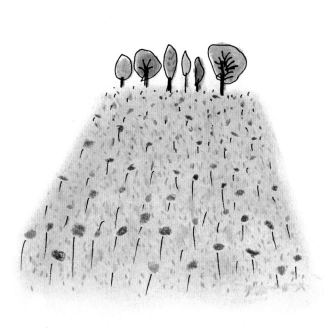

MY FRIEND

My friend is like bark
rounding a tree
he warms like sun
on a winter day
he cools like water
in the hot noon
his voice is ready
as a spring bird
he is my friend
and I am his

EMILY HEARN

WITH A FRIEND...

The mere sense of contiguity is a delight....
sunshine comes, the air is clearer,
there is more life in it,
the flowers grow more beautifully,
the sky is fairer,
and the night is deeper.
All the earth grows glad; and there
is a new note in the song of the birds.

M.J. SAVAGE

CHINESE OATH OF FRIENDSHIP

I want to be your friend
For ever and ever without break or decay.
When the hills are all flat
And the rivers are all dry,
When it lightens and thunders in winter,
When it rains and snows in summer,
When Heaven and Earth mingle
Not till then will I part from you.

CHINESE, 1ST CENTURY

FRIENDSHIP, A DEAR BALM....

A SMILE AMONG DARK FROWNS:

A BELOVED LIGHT:

A SOLITUDE,

A REFUGE, A DELIGHT.

PERCY BYSSHE SHELLEY (1792–1822)

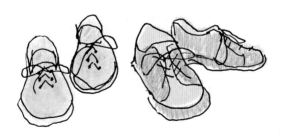

The weary miles
         pass swiftly,
    taken in a joyous stride.
And all the world
        seems brighter,
    when a friend walks
        by our side.

AUTHOR UNKNOWN

*Wherever you are
it is your own friends
who make your world.*

WILLIAM JAMES (1842–1910)

...friendship only is, indeed, genuine
when two friends,
without speaking a word to each other,
can, nevertheless, find happiness
in being together.

GEORG EBERS (1837–1898)

*Silences and distances
are woven into the texture
of every true friendship.*

ROBERTA ISRAELOFF

A million billion words
have been spoken
about what friendship means
but two good friends can be together
without speaking a single word
and know precisely
what friendship means.

STUART AND LINDA MACFARLANE

THOSE SPECIAL FRIENDS
WHOM I AM CLOSEST TO...
INTEREST ME:
HOW THEY THINK,
WHAT THEY FEEL,
HOW THEY DEAL WITH LIFE —
ITS GIFTS AND ITS DENIALS.
THEY ADD TO AND COMPLETE
THE CIRCLE OF MY LIFE
AND ENRICH ME.

LAUREN BACALL, B.1924

What's the fun
of an adventure
if you can't share
it with a friend?

PAM BROWN, B.1928

We feel more deeply,
remember more clearly,
enjoy events with greater pleasure
if we have a friend to share with.

PAMELA DUGDALE

*Grief can take care of itself,
but to get the full value of a joy
you must have somebody
to divide it with.*

MARK TWAIN (1835–1910)

WE WHO HAVE FRIENDS
ARE WRAPPED AROUND IN KINDLINESS
AND SAFE FROM THE COLD
IMMENSITY OF SPACE.

PAM BROWN, B.1928

*...many of us are more dependent
than at any other time in history
upon friendships that truly work for us,
bring us joy and give us
a sense of well-being and belonging.*

ADELAIDE BRY

A friend is there for you when
absolutely no one else is.

PAM BROWN, B.1928

A REAL FRIEND IS ONE
WHO WALKS IN
WHEN THE REST OF THE WORLD
WALKS OUT.

WALTER WINCHELL (1897–1972)

What do we live for,
if it is not
to make life less difficult for each other?

GEORGE ELIOT (MARY ANN EVANS)

✳ ✳

HOW OFTEN HAVE WE BUILT EACH OTHER
AS SHELTERS AGAINST THE COLD.

AUDRE LORDE (1934–1992)

Our friendships are... the structures
that hold us in place when our world
threatens to dissolve.

ROSALYN CHISSICK,
FROM "NEW WOMAN", AUGUST 1994

All the others sit beside the beds
and bring chrysanthemums
and magazines and bananas.
You bring me enormous balloons
and jokes and Ella tapes and melons.
And the latest detective story.
And yourself.
Thank you, thank you, thank you!!

PAM BROWN, B.1928

Oh, the comfort – the inexpressible
comfort of feeling safe with a person
– having neither to weigh thoughts
nor measure words,
but pouring them
all right out,
just as they are chaff and grain together;
knowing that a faithful hand
will take and sift them,
keep what is worth keeping,
and then with the breath of kindness
blow the rest away.

DINAH MARIA MULOCK CRAIK (1826–1887),
FROM "A LIFE FOR A LIFE"

They are closest to us
who best understand what life
means to us, who feel for us
as we feel for ourselves,
who are bound to us
in triumph and disaster,
who break the spell of our loneliness.

HENRY ALONZO MYERS

*...It is that my friends
have made the story of my life.
In a thousand ways
they have turned my limitations
into beautiful privileges,
and enabled me
to walk serene and happy
in the shadow cast by my deprivation.*

HELEN KELLER (1880–1968)

Happy is the house

that shelters a friend!

RALPH WALDO EMERSON (1803–1882)

*"Stay" is a charming word
in a friend's vocabulary.*

LOUISA MAY ALCOTT (1832–1888)

Friendship is what shows us
that we are not alone
in any joy or any sorrow.

PAM BROWN, B.1928

Friends are all that matter.

GELETT BURGESS (1866–1951)

Friendship is the only cement
that will ever hold
the world together.

WOODROW WILSON (1856–1924)

The Beatles knew what they were about
when they wrote their song,
"I'll get by with a little help from my friends".
How else would any of us get by
without this stretching out of hands
to friends, neighbours, nations?

KAY DICK

GIRL FRIENDS

Girl friends have bigger telephone bills
than Hollywood tycoons.

. . .

A discussion between girl friends
about which cinema to go to invariably
ends up with them staying home,
watching a video of "Pride and Prejudice",
and a major decision on a change of career.

PAM BROWN, B.1928

*Friends are people who go
on conspiratorial shopping sprees together,
diving in and out of shops
totally beyond their price range,
and ending up eating
oozing cream cakes
with only just enough money to get home.*

CHARLOTTE GRAY, B.1937

*When you need to whine
about things going wrong,
when you need to moan
about life's little injustices,
a friend is happy
just to listen to your tales of woe.*

LINDA MACFARLANE

Your knock.
Your face at the window.
No need to rush around,
        shoving things under cushions.
No need for guilt that the ironing's
        teetering on the chair.
No need for the best cups.
No need for regrets
that there are only broken crackers left.
        "Come in. I'll put the kettle on."
"Now – what's your news?"

CHARLOTTE GRAY, B.1937

My friend and I tell each other
all our worries.
Often there is nothing
we can do to solve them.
But knowing
that we are there for each other,
prepared to listen,
is all the help we need.

LINDA MACFARLANE, B.1953

To others,
we will be seen as two old biddies
kicking off their shoes,
dumping down shopping bags,
choosing lethal pastries.
But to each other we are ourselves,
a little scarred by the passing years,
but still the girls
who shared a bag of toffee
on the playground wall,
we at least are not deceived
by skin, spectacles and silvery hair.

PAM BROWN, B.1928

Long friendships are like jewels,
        polished over time
to become beautiful and enduring.

CELIA BRAYFIELD,
FROM "WOMAN AND HOME", OCT. 97

*Surely there is no more beautiful sight
to see in all this world...
    than the growth of two friends' natures
    who, as they grow old together,
are always fathoming with newer needs,
    deeper depths of each other's life....*

PHILLIPS BROOKS

To the young, friendship comes
as the glory of the spring,
a very miracle of beauty,
a mystery of birth:
to the old it has the bloom of autumn,
beautiful still.

HUGH BLACK

AT EVERY STAGE OF MY LIFE
FRIENDSHIP HAS BEEN THE MAIN SOURCE
OF MY QUITE
OUTRAGEOUSLY
ENJOYABLE EXISTENCE.

SIR GEOFFREY KEYNES

Happiness
is the whole world as friends.
It's light all through
your life.

DANIEL DILLING, AGE 8

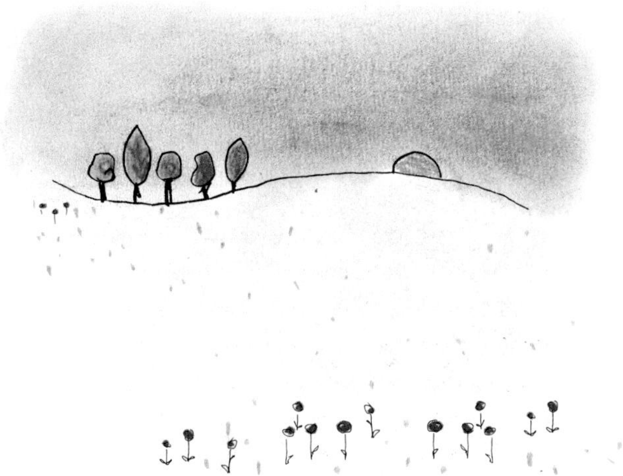

*Deft thieves can break your locks
and carry off your savings,
fire consume your home...
– fortune can't take away what
you give friends:
that wealth stays yours forever.*

MARCUS MARTIAL (C.40–C.104)

FRIENDS ARE PATIENT AND KIND,
THEY ARE NOT JEALOUS OR BOASTFUL,
THEY ARE NOT ARROGANT OR RUDE.

FRIENDSHIP BEARS ALL THINGS,
BELIEVES ALL THINGS,
HOPES ALL THINGS, ENDURES ALL THINGS.

FRIENDSHIP NEVER ENDS.

ADAPTED FROM 1 CORINTHIANS 1:13

What is the opposite of two?
A lonely me, a lonely you.

RICHARD WILBUR, B.1921

A friend may move away – so far that you
may never meet again.
And yet they are a part of you forever.

PAM BROWN, B.1928

*Your friendship has been the sunlight
that has transformed my days.*

PAM BROWN, B.1928

There's nothing worth
the wear of winning,
But laughter and the love of friends.

HILAIRE BELLOC (1870–1953)

* *

MY FRIENDSHIP
WITH YOU
WAS — IS —
THE GREAT BLESSING
OF MY LIFE.

JULIA WEDGEWOOD

Because I got you to look after me,
and you got me to look after you....
We got each other,
that's what....

JOHN STEINBECK (1902–1968)

Helen Exley runs her own publishing company which sells giftbooks in more than seventy countries. She had always wanted to do a little book on smiles, and has been collecting the quotations for many years, but always felt that the available illustrations just weren't quite right. Then Helen fell in love with Joanna Kidney's happy, bright pictures and knew immediately they had the feel she was looking for. She asked Joanna to work on *smile*, and then to go on to contribute the art for four more books: *friend*, *happy day!*, *love* and *hope! dream!*

Joanna Kidney lives in County Wicklow in Ireland. She juggles her time between working on various illustration projects and producing her own art for shows and exhibitions. Her whole range of greeting cards *Joanna's Pearlies* – some of which appear in this book – won the prestigious 2001 Henries oscar for 'best fun or graphic range'.

Acknowledgements: The publishers are grateful for permission to reproduce copyright material. Whilst every reasonable effort has been made to trace copyright holders, the publishers would be pleased to hear from any not here acknowledged. EMILY HEARN: "My Friend" from *Hockey Cards and Hopscotch*, by John McInnes and Emily Hearn. Published by Nelson Canada. Used with permission. I CHING, or *Book of Changes*: Translated by Richard Wilhelm, copyright © 1967, renewed 1995. Reprinted by permission of Princeton University Press and Heinrich Hugendubel Verlag GmbH. ELIZABETH JENNINGS: From "Friendship" from *Collected Poems* by Elizabeth Jennings, published by Carcanet. **IMPORTANT COPYRIGHT NOTICE: PAM BROWN, PAMELA DUGDALE, CHARLOTTE GRAY, STUART AND LINDA MACFARLANE © Helen Exley 2003.**